*To My Fellow Supe
With Love
Judy x*

HeavenRead.Com

Judy Dyer

This Book is a mixture of
Reason, Belief, Expression, True Oneness,
Acknowledgement & Honesty.
A book of anecdotes

First published by Barny Books
All rights reserved

No part of this publication may be reproduced or transmitted in any way or by any means, including electronic storage and retrieval, without prior permission of the publisher.

ISBN No: 978.1.906542.22.1

Publishers:	Barny Books
	Hough on the Hill
	Grantham
	Lincolnshire
	NG32 2BB

	Tel: 01400 250246
	www.barnybooks.biz

Acknowledgements:

A heartfelt thank you to Stephen for designing the cover for HeavenRead.Com

Dedicated to

my daughter Celine

Information

This book offers real live evidence of circumstances and I am now running courses to reinforce the evidence of how different life can be in the positive sense ...
see the web site www.bcdays.com for more information.

I am available to give talks to different groups ...
look at www.heavenread.com or www.judydyer.co.uk

Remember:

**Seek not to change the World
but change how You see the World**

HeavenRead.Com

Foreword

1. Never Give Up
2. Bringing Heaven to Earth, Why Wait?
3. A Brave Move
4. A Toast To YOU
5. Are YOU Choosing
6. Watching or Waiting
7. From The Heart
8. Going Beyond Fear
9. In The Now
10. Likening to a Lily (Which flower...)
11. Our Type?
12. Your Prince has Come
13. Baby Love
14. Glamour & Glitz
15. Poison Ivy
16. Millionaires Row
17. Relatively Speaking
18. Dancing Queen
19. My Wondrous Story
20. Taking Off the Mask
21. If I only had Time
22. Proud Mum of a Proud Mum
23. Dream On
24. Sink or Swim
25. Pushing Your Buttons
26. Roadmap or Sat Nav

Conclusion

Foreword

Welcome

When the messages came for me to write a book, they came fast and furious. All within the space of a few days.
They say, (whoever *they* are), be careful what you ask for and what you put out you will attract. Well I seem to have attracted plenty of things I never knew I asked for. Boring my life is not … I must have asked for them in my sleep ... or is it my Karma?

This is a book based on some of my life's experience and philosophy in a hope it will help others to move through their life knowing you can always make a difference and never call off the search for your hopes and dreams.

It took me so many years to learn, but what I was searching for was already inside me and that to be full and whole was already there, well at least the foundations were...
Realisation is a wonderful thing. It's a pity many of us don't recognise what's inside us and what we are truly capable of.

Remember, you can't Love Yourself until you Know Yourself.

Enjoy.

Judy

1. Never give Up

In this ever changing world, especially the one we live in today, everything revolves around money and survival – dog eat dog and man eat man, well that's how it feels to me. Everybody's trying to sell you something from mortgages to Viagra and, pardon me, but it's a load of balls whichever way you look at it. As a single woman, aiming to live a decent quality of life and willing to work, life becomes more challenging every day. Luckily I'm the sort of person who bounces back 95% of the time. My glass is mostly half full – usually with wine if left to me! I've three marriages behind me and I can't say failed because all three have taught me something and hey, I like dressing up and being the centre of attention. Not for me, "I learned the truth at seventeen" as in the Janis Ian song - Ugly duckling I was not willing to settle for...

It's not that I meant to stay single; the reality is that I'm not willing to stay where I'm not happy. I know life is a compromise and that over the years I've become more tolerant but I'm a huge romantic and I do believe that you can make life more exciting every day and not just now and again. I have a wonderful friend who is 25 years older than me and she taught me however bad things are. there's always time to have a laugh and a gin and tonic. Her name is Jean and her best friend is called Sheila. We call them Jean and Tonic and that is just what they are, a real tonic. Their motto is, "Is it gin o clock yet?" They're always inspirational and always have a story to tell.

We've laughed, cried and got merry together on many occasions. My sanity owes them a lot, as I do to all my wonderful friends I have met over the years, the ones that stayed, the ones that left and the ones I've yet to know.

People come into your life for a reason, usually to meet a need. They are there for the reason you need them to be, to give you support or guidance – to help you spiritually or emotionally and, when your need is addressed, they will walk away. This is a beautiful poem by an unknown called, P*eople Come Into Your Life for a Reason* and was sent to me when I was going through a difficult time.

People come into your life for a reason, a season or a lifetime.
When you know which one it is, you will know what to do for that person.
When someone is in your life for a REASON, it is usually to meet a need you have expressed.
They have come to assist you through a difficulty, to provide you with guidance and support, to aid you physically, emotionally or spiritually. They may seem like a godsend and they are. They are there for the reason you need them to be.
Then, without any wrongdoing on your part or at an inconvenient time, this person will say or do something to bring the relationship to an end.
Sometimes they die. Sometimes they walk away. Sometimes they act up and force you to take a stand.
What we must realize is that our need has been met, our desire fulfilled, their work is done.
The prayer you sent up has been answered and now it is time to move on.

2. Bringing Heaven to Earth

So my title …. HeavenRead.Com

Stairway to Heaven or highway to Hell!
Which is yours??

We all look forward to when we leave this life, hoping for a smidgeon of a chance of going to heaven,

What thoughts do we conjure up…?
Do we think total peace and tranquillity, no worries, free of pain - physical and mental, free choice? - A welcome committee. Nothing to prove. No ego battles with yourself or anyone, no bills...only karmic ones of course...
Pity we can't send an email to God@heavenmail.com
If you were a miracle would you want to give yourself to a person that didn't believe in miracles? Do we really have to pass an acid test and be questioned by St Peter at the heavenly gates?

When we are in total equilibrium you can hear yourself quoting, "Oh that's heaven" but how can we quote about somewhere we've never been or is that where we came from? - The Source and *that* is why we feel so separate and isolated when we don't report in!! (meaning meditation or prayer or whatever works for you).

What's your idea of heaven? It's probably different for each of us. I'd be soooo interested to hear YOUR ideas. After all we're all in this together... the good, the bad and the ugly

So what would *your* question be in your email?

And do you wake up and think I'm glad to be alive or do you say, here we go again? It doesn't have to be like that.

Life's a party from now on because the war that's going on is right between our ears. Rather than let circumstances control our thoughts, let's turn it around and let thoughts control our circumstances.

We are what we focus on, so if you focus on what you haven't got, that's what you will attract *but,* if you focus on what you already have and feel *gratitude,* that's what you will receive. You will be **amazed** how things *can* turn around. A simple example was when my friend came around one Sunday for us to go out. I asked if she fancied going to our favourite bar/restaurant. She said, "Yes" so I duly phoned to be told they weren't accepting any more bookings. A few days earlier I had been to a refurbished restaurant and had the business card in my bag.
I asked my friend if she fancied trying out this new restaurant instead. "Yes," she said, putting her trust in my judgement. I telephoned, reserved a table and took her along. We not only got the best seat in the house but my friend said she had driven by this restaurant only two days before and thought how nice it would be to go there as it looked so inviting. If she had thought, 'I'm never going anywhere like that,' guess what would have happened - nothing and that's the way it works!

3. A Brave Move

It was a very brave move when my soul decided to incarnate.

Why I wanted to swim that fast and beat all the other million sperm that was swimming for literally dear life escapes me... Whatever the reason it must have stayed with me because I only like swimming in warm water, mainly the Caribbean or the Indian Ocean but real life keeps getting in the way. Although I work at the local leisure centre and have done now for over 23 years teaching aerobics, I never fancy swimming in the municipal water. The 23 years of working out has paid off though. I still keep thinking someone is going to spot me and sign me up for a modelling career so I don't need to get out of bed for less than £3,000 per day. Sadly this is not the case and I'm begging the bank to reconsider the mortgage deal. Hey ho. Get back in the real world. I will never stop dreaming. Live the dream, as they say in the United States! What do they say in the UK? There'll always be an England - or will there? Not with all the influx of foreign blood that's pouring in. I hear more foreign voices than British! No disrespect to the foreigners but it's just getting a little crowded. After all most of us procreate.

Get a job with a good pension... That's another one. I know I would make a fantastic Prime Minister and boy, oh boy, I'd sort the men out from the boys and the wheat from the chaff and the wasters taking advantage... Would I!

And the Credit Crunch. What a joke! ...Talk about a false sense of security... Encouraging us to Spend. Spend, Spend and then they want it back and say we're in a recession.
In an ideal world there wouldn't be any wars. What's the point? A few men in power fighting for territory, (that's

what it all boils down to) who want to be in charge and rule the world. Every being that's a victim of war is a child being born to some mother and any mother wouldn't dream of killing a child that has grown inside her and she has given birth to, apart from mine!!! (And that's another story). We are *all* someone's baby and someone's child.... So instead of sending our men to war send them to help share our knowledge and resources. Let's make a difference for the good of humanity.

4. A Toast to You

How often have you toasted yourself for your achievement? The majority of us under-estimate our abilities about what we do achieve from day to day... But if you get up and begin thinking, 'what can I *give* to the day' instead of 'what can I *get* from the day' I'm sure you will find that your days will be quite different...

First smile at yourself in the mirror. Give yourself some encouragement…..

Get up 5 minutes earlier and do **five** minutes improving something about you! It maybe checking your posture, it may be a self affirmation. Send me an email if you don't know what an affirmation is or Google it. Or, buy Louise Hay's daily calendar of affirmations... (Self Talk In a Nutshell).

It may be pampering your skin. Two to three minutes skin brushing with some great body lotion... a good stretch, anything to make you feeeeel good... Phone someone and give them something good to think about... Make someone else's day.

Have a glass of hot water and lemon to wake up your insides, maybe crush in some ginger, I crush mine in the garlic press, and a touch of cayenne pepper stirred in. My mini daily detox...

Detox your thoughts by telling all the bad ones to clear off or words to that effect. We are a result of our thoughts. What we think about today, we will attract tomorrow.

Next, have a nourishing breakfast even if it's a smoothie. Something nice and quick would be a cocktail of fruit juice, vitamin tablet, a piece of fruit and some protein powder to kick start your body. Whizz it round in a blender. It only takes 2 minutes.

You wouldn't get very far in your car without fuel but your body needs it and its relying on YOU, yes YOU ......
Speaking of cars I bet most blokes spend more time on their car than they do on their bodies and expect them to perform to peak performance. Well guess what, if you put crap in, you'll get crap out... You could liken it to a sausage machine. You can't expect to put beef in and get pork sausages out or for you veggies you can't expect to put vegetables in and get soya beans out... And it's the same in life.

We put doubt, worry, apprehension, guilt, anxiety in and expect to get success happiness and euphoria out.

We incorporate the sausage machine in our 5 day courses. It's amazing how you can change your whole perspective on life after this course. Email me for more details or check out my website www.bcdays.com. So change your eating habits and your thinking habits and your life *will* change for the better!!

5. Are you Choosing

What would you hang on to most - a compliment or a criticism? Mostly the answer is - a criticism because you can't get it out of your mind.

YET.... If you asked someone what they would choose - they'd say the opposite... So why aren't we choosing...??

If we're having an awful day half the time, it's how we choose to react to things that dictates how we feel. Yes it might be raining. Yes the car might not start and yeah, someone yells at you. Yes you're in a traffic jam, but guess what YOU ARE the traffic. People seem to forget that... yes the gas bill and telephone bill have just arrived... but that's life... A telephone is your communication. The gas central heating keeps us warm. We're so reliant on our cars. We've probably not asked our partner how they are this morning, given them a smile, done something nice for them and started the day off beautifully...

Enjoy the feeling of waking. What's the alternative? Enjoy the water cleansing your body in the shower. Take a few moments in the silence. Be aware of your breathing slow and controlled. Have a good stretch- your body <u>will</u> love you for it.

And leave the house smiling and carry it with you, believe me its infectious. If you're feeling rubbish - remember the last thing that did make you smile... there must be something..!

Something?

6. Watching and Waiting doc

If you could remember your very first vivid memory what would that be? I would hope it would be one that you will cherish!

I remember mine, it was being taken to the hospital at 3 years old with my head gaping open and being at the hospital with my father having been sent for from work and the nurse talking me through having stitches in my head….. My mother said I'd fallen off the sofa whilst playing with my baby brother.

I sort of remember my brother being born just before and my mother having him at home and a faint memory of my Mum's Mother, Eileen being around and who also had a baby a month after my brother Geoff was born. She died soon after. She would only be 39 and died of cancer. The baby was adopted by the father and his new partner. The baby's name was Helen and will be a month older than me. I remember visiting her once. She lived in Calverton in Nottingham.

It was a very dreary place where we lived. My parents had moved there after living in rented rooms in a terraced house in Ilkeston in Derbyshire on Manners Street. My parents had to live there after a whirlwind shotgun wedding.

We moved shortly after to a place called Crompton Street in Ilkeston. I remember my Dad sitting me on his knee in an old car around the back, no idea where the car came from...

This is now a famous street which was quoted and shown in a documentary with Robert Lindsay the actor recently. He originates from the Ilkeston, Derbyshire region... I wrote to him once asking if I could be an extra in his film but was turned down. I must look out the letter...

My parents were not very popular with my Dad's parents having ended up with me after a naughty weekend whilst my grandparents were away; apparently they were both virgins, my parents I mean. They both worked together at a bed factory called Beauvale and then my dad bedded my mother and along came Judith Ann Weston.

They say you ask to be born to the parents you requested before arriving on the planet, God only knows what I was thinking of, LITERALLY, I'M INTERESTED TO GO BACK AND FIND OUT WHY. I must have needed to learn or put many things right from my past lives. MY Karma! Ahhhhhhhhhhh....

What's your Karma...?

Do you feel you have a mission for this life or are you still trying to figure it out?
.

7. From the heart

Working from the heart, how much treasure is in your treasure chest? What about sweet heart! You don't say 'Hi sweet head' you say 'Hi, sweet heart'.

How about 'she broke my heart' not 'he' or 'she broke my head' although we say he or she is doing my head in.

Heart breaker - Not head breaker. !

Where does our hand go when we talk about something or someone close to us? Our hand goes straight to the heart... When something's annoying you they say it's all in your head!!! Why is this? It is the Heart that is felt not the head.

Home is where the heart is and the real home is inside yourself. You can create whatever you want if you go inside yourself. You can be as imaginary as you like its unique only to you…. And only you can invite someone in to share it.

So open your heart to yourself and then invite others in at your leisure. You'll be pleased you did.

Keeping it closed keeps you in a *very* lonely place!

8. Going Beyond Fear

Just BEeeee............
How often do you think Life's not going My Way?
Have you ever REALLY thought why that is?
It feels like you're pushing a rope uphill or swimming against the tide and that no one understands how you feeeeeel.

When it really gets too much for some people they opt out, have a nervous breakdown and attempt, or even commit suicide, but ......this is a case of mistaken identity. That's not who you really are.

Never think that you're not good enough. Good enough for whom?

Never think that you're not successful enough.... that nobody loves you. ... We have to lose the attachment and start looking in the right filing cabinet.

For instance..............If you want love, success, wealth, happiness and you're looking at i.e. the wrong person, the wrong job, mixing with the wrong people, then all you are doing is looking in the wrong filing cabinet.

So why are YOU choosing to keep looking there?

If you want eggs, milk and juice you go to the fridge not the microwave. If you want meat you go to the butchers not the bakers, and so on...

If you could choose (which you can!) then go and look in the other filing cabinet... It's so simple.
The sun is always above the clouds. It's just that it is obscured and that's where your happiness sometimes lies.

Know the clouds will clear and the blue sky is ALWAYS there.

Lose the attachment to the fear…

Sometimes we feel it is safer to hang on. It's like a living hell but what if we let go, where will we go?

Dare to dream…You will always get what you expect… and what you resist persists…

The definition of faith is what you can't see yet. Belief is a powerful thing… Liken it to a spiritual diet…

If you really want to look at courage watch the video about Johnny, The Boy whose skin fell off. (An amazing film) This true story really puts it into perspective about getting what you want! And also makes you take stock of what really matters.

Why is it always in the face of adversity that we truly learn our most valuable life lessons?

So what do we do? A friend of mine has just come back from a Byron Katie workshop. Katie asked them all to go out into the garden and ask the first thing that their eyes alighted on, a question regarding their most serious problem that they felt they couldn't solve, and people were coming in with profound messages. Then this guy stood up and said that the first thing he saw was a bee on the floor. He asked it his most serious question and the universe answered him........Just Bee! Get it! So don't worry about anything - just BE.
It sounds so simple but all the answers are inside us waiting to be accessed! We always think they're somewhere else…

9. In the Now

Living in the now is so powerful.

You've heard the saying 'yesterdays history, tomorrow's a mystery and today's a gift. That's why they call it the present', and indeed it is.

I have been teaching myself not to waver over the past, good or bad. If it's bad it robs you of the now and the future hasn't happened yet because tomorrow is always the present when it comes. So you need to embrace the moment and, if you find yourself drifting into either, (yesterday or tomorrow) take a few deep conscious breaths and bring yourself back into the NOW. It's very powerful. I don't mean to not plan or remember, but bring the planning into the NOW or bring the past into the NOW, into the moment…. And then let it go …

Remember that anything in the past cannot, I emphasize, CANNOT hurt you not unless we allow it to because *we are* in charge of our feelings ….

Because it's gone and behind you, it's up to us how we choose to feel about it.

I have had many a conversation and even said it myself, "He (or she) really …hurt me or hurt my feelings". It shows how we react to each individual situation… Nobody hurts us unless it's physical. We hurt ourselves by HOW we react to each situation so it is situational…

The other person supposedly hurting us is doing what they choose to do and do not give a jot to how it would affect us or me as the case may be. But it's when we find out that we allow it to hurt us and then we're the victim and we go into victim mode, and they say I never meant to hurt you. What baloney. Would you really choose to be with someone like that?

So we're choosing again…!!!!

If you could really choose your life how would it be?
Take some time to write out your ideal day ….
What would be your dream day?
Then why aren't you living it?

Once I listened to a CD programme and it questioned, 'If you could be anybody in the world, who would that be?'
And then the second question was, 'If you could live anywhere in the world where would that be?'
The third question, 'If you could choose your ideal partner who would that be?'

The next question was - then why aren't you doing all three? It's because we're not choosing and most of us are still looking in the wrong filing cabinets...

<u>Wrong file (Looking In)</u>
Despair
Doubt
I'm not good enough. Not worthy
Can I really do it?
I feel rubbish

<u>Right file (Expecting)</u>
Success
Happiness
Wealth
Fulfilment
Peace

But each one of us is where we are because of our belief systems

If you think you can - you can.
If you think you can't, you can't and what stand's in the way. One lousy comma and a letter. So it's how we feel that counts. We don't really learn things from words but more so how the words make us feel.

Words are just words. Syllables upon syllables.

You need to internalise your feelings...

That's where the answers lie... Most of us are looking and constantly looking externally when the answer lies inside us... The answers always lie within us. When I receive one of those 'ah, ha' moments I joke with my friends that 'It's the direct line' (my direct line to the universe). The thing is it's true, we silently say give me the answer to a problem and one usually pops up.

All you need to do is Ask.

10. Likening to a Lily (Which flower are You?)

The flowering lily is perfection personified to me. It's pure, beautiful, fragrant, proud with an everlasting beauty. I always have lilies in my house and would like everybody to send me them not only when I die but all through my living days. I feel they are so spiritual and every time I see one it lifts my spirits.

If I could liken myself to any flower, this would be the one. I like most flowers except perhaps chrysanthemums. They remind me of sedate old ladies and flower shows and I don't really know why … maybe my great aunt had them, no offence meant if you love chrysanthemums.

For you it might be a fragrant rose with its soft petals and enigmatic scent. A spiritual practice I read about recently really resonated with me and is practiced by the wise sages called the heart of the rose. To perform this practice all you need is a fresh rose and a silent place. Stare into the centre of the rose, its heart. Notice its colour and texture, savour its fragrance and only think about the rose. Your mind will wander but keep bringing it back. Spend 5 minutes a day doing this. It will seem hard at first but perseverance will help to train and quieten your mind... Make it a daily exercise for one week...

Or it could be a daffodil. On one of the courses I attended we likened people to daffodils and likened daffodils to people. In relation to a daffodil, some people live in the dark or in the light. So imagine if you were a daffodil and had just pushed through the surface of the soil and spoke to your fellow daffodil and said "Wow, isn't it fantastic?" explaining all you could see on this wonderful earth. Sorry, but it's not with you because your fellow daffodil comrade was still just below the surface and not reached its destination... So it's a bit like people really some of us live above ground and some below... A fellow student on the course explained it to her 5 year old who took it all on board. The next day she saw her next door neighbours approaching the house who were pretty miserable folk. Having picked up on this the 5 year old called out to her mummy and said "Mummy, Mummy it's the underground people from next door"... out of the mouths of babes!!!

So what flower are you and how would you epitomise yourself and why ....? And how fragrant are you? Maybe you're a prickly bush...!!

11. Our type!!

When I was 26 years old I kept thinking, as many of us do, I deserve more and what is my purpose……..

I was working in Debenhams department store in a very mundane job but was full of inspiration and believed that I could work my way up the ladder. I worked with a colleague who I greatly admired. I aspired to be just like her.

At the time I had a boyfriend, Barry who absolutely adored me. He worked for the same company where my husband was, working on computers when computers were really coming into their own … My husband (Alan) and I were estranged at this time.

I had met Barry at a works evening function at a Go Kart Fun Park. I thought he was very amusing. He reminded me of Leo Sayer. He was cute. I couldn't wear heels when I went out with him though - he was too short. Anyway I bumped into him again at a Donington Grand Prix Race meeting that my girlfriend, Pauline had asked me to go with her as there was this guy she was seeing. Barry was surprised that I had broken up with Alan. Little did he know he was an incessant drinker and sometimes didn't come home all night. He gave me a lift home in the gold XJS Jaguar car he had been allocated for a month for achieving top salesman in the company. The next morning he telephoned me and that was it. He was besotted and I was enjoying the full attention. He took me out for lunch the next day at the local Novotel which had a pool. It was very fashionable at the time. Within a couple of days after bumping into him, he gave me a card which said all over it magnificent fabulous, magnificent fabulous... Someone thought I was magnificent and fabulous and had the courage to let me know. Wow, was I flattered and it really boosted my confidence..!!!!!!!!!!!!! I had been devoid of compliments most of my life... Well talk about admiration society. I couldn't get enough of it flattery, wining, dining, constant telephone calls and looking at me with complete adoration.... I was lapping it up!! And he was like a lap puppy. There was one small problem... He was married...

Moving slightly forward and proceeding to my first divorce and still enjoying the flattery of Barry, I used to frequent a pub called The Hemlock Stone. It was a real friendly classy pub with a lot of NICE people in there.... Tony was one of them, a director at the local Players factory and he became more than a close friend...

I used to meet up with a small crowd midweek and always on a Sunday. There was one particular guy who used to come in who was always very generous with his friends and seemed to have his own entourage in the corner. I didn't pay much attention to them and was in the sister pub (The Admiral Rodney) up the road one evening, which was the bees knees in pubs and one where I had worked for a short time as a barmaid, that was when the afore mentioned gent Chris fought through the very crowded pub where I was having a drink with my friend Pauline and asked if I would go out for a drink with him one night. I was so surprised and said I would despite my friend saying, 'He's not your type' to which I replied no but, hey ho, whatever, it's just a bit of fun ......!!!

So what is my type...!!!
Or what is your type? ...
And why do we even have a type... ....
Write it down in the notes at the back of the book.

12. Your Prince has come

Well I did go on the date with Chris and again got treated admirably and somehow going out with Chris was like those childhood dreams. When we're growing up and dreaming of being grown up, how many of us are hoping to marry our prince or princess?

Chris continued wooing me and I felt like a princess and he sent me a card quoting, "You have kissed many frogs in your life but now your prince has come!" (What a cliché) Just for the record he sent it to his next wife as well. I'd come home and there were little Harrods hampers on my doorstep and mini bottles of champagne from Fortnum & Mason and flowers would arrive at work and at home. Telemessages which were very much in fashion then (like telegrams on a lovely card), requests on the radio, telephone messages asking me to meet him in a restaurant and a taxi sent for me. He also enrolled me in a top private health club. I was on a whirlwind tour and for someone like me who had a very simple upbringing, it was great, and I felt <u>very</u> special. (And shouldn't we all!!)

By this time I was working in the local John Lewis Store (the reason I took it was that I had followed my mentor with whom I had been working in Debenhams so that I could follow in her footsteps and be management material….). Well of course some people don't want you to become management and equal to them. They like you where they want you. I used to hang on to her every word... She was about 13 years my senior, very glamorous, and a go getter. I even used to drive her to work and back. One evening we were walking to the car park and one of the other managers was asking why she travelled with me. Her reply was, "You don't have a dog and bark yourself". That cut me to the bone. I was just a dogsbody... From that day on my feelings altered...

The universe works in mysterious ways. As you will find out...

Well not only was I getting lots of attention from Chris, my other boyfriend Barry was getting nervous that someone else was vying for my attention... So presents and flowers also started to arrive from him...

What I didn't know was that Chris had arranged to take himself off for a month to the Marbella Club in the January; a trip he had promised himself after his estranged wife of the time had turned down a month in Switzerland. At that time all I knew was Marbella was somewhere in Spain and thought he was off to some ordinaire holiday club. Didn't have Google in those days!!!! Even the post cards he sent didn't do it any justice...

If you're not familiar with the Marbella Club, it used to and still is one of the most prestigious holiday destinations in the World!!

Well he'd only been gone a few hours when he called playing romantic music down the phone and I'd politely have to listen and he'd just say did you enjoy that? - I'd say yes. I can't quite remember the artiste now. It wasn't Julio, someone Spanish but similar... Apparently after the two weeks his telephone bill was about £400 pounds, a lot of dosh back then. A few days into his holiday he telephoned to ask if I would like to join him for a couple of weeks. I said I had an allocation of a week's holiday in February and he guided me to his travel agent to make the arrangement... and arranged to send me some cash!!

When I told Barry that I was considering a few days away to clear my head he came to take me for lunch and decided to surprise me with an airline ticket to guess where - yes Spain, the same week. So there I was with two tickets to go to two separate locations on the Costa del Sol…

Well talk about surprise, I don't think gobsmacked was in fashion then. I went back to work totally wobbled... What was I to do....? Well after much deliberation I decided to go and visit Chris, after all he asked me first….When I told Barry that I wasn't going, there were heated discussions and lots of tears… but, wait for it, Barry turned up not taking no for an answer and begged me to go with him. He looked so white and desperate that I thought it was easier to phone Chris and tell him that I wouldn't be joining him. So I ended up going with Barry….. (Didn't work out) I couldn't move a muscle on the holiday without being questioned. Our first holiday and our last….

When I came back from my 'holiday' with Barry, I heard from my best friend that Chris had cut his holiday short to come home. Of course I wasn't there... So I telephoned Chris, thinking he probably wouldn't still be interested. I was wrong. He invited me to his new abode and when I arrived he held me for about ten minutes on the doorstep - which is a long time bearing in mind it was February… And his words were "I never want to let you go"……

So my advice to you would be to always follow your instinct. You'll be glad you did...

P.S. I did go to The Marbella Club and I can highly recommend it!!

A few weeks later, having a great time and loving it, things were getting more difficult at work and all sorts of bizarre

things happened. My manager in question deemed to organise discrepancies and other things to make sure that the finger pointed at me...This became quite upsetting. The day of my birthday came and Chris dropped me off and said, "I'll meet you after work and expect a surprise."
I'd no sooner set foot on my department when I was told I had been summoned up to the Store manager's office. I thought, 'What now?'!!! Anyway it was another made up story with which I had to deal with. The day continued and I kept my spirits up... Flowers and gifts arrived, much to the annoyance of certain parties...

After work my colleague and I collected our items and gifts from security. We walked out on to the busy street outside and there in the middle of the street holding up all the traffic was a White Rolls Royce.

Clare said, "I bet's that's for you."
"Don't be daft" I said, "Chris has an XJS, why would he send a roller?" The windows in the roller were smoked so we couldn't see who was inside. Anyway, still holding up the traffic a chauffeur stepped out and started walking over to me and asked if I was Judy.
"Yes", I said.
"Well, please let me take your gifts. I've come to take you home..."
And then the window went down and there was Chris in the back... smiling... Clare waved me off but the best bit was both the managers who had been treating me quite abominably were both standing at the door... Was I feeling smug? You bet!
I thought this is it. I can't go back there again, so arranged an appointment with the HR Manager the next week and gave in my notice. What did I say about the Universe?!!! Works in very mysterious ways...

13. Baby Love

Chris and I stayed together and eventually moved in together, having a lovely time travelling all over the world for around five years. And then I found out I was pregnant!

When I found out I was having a baby, you could have knocked me down with a feather. Literally! Surely not, I was on the pill and had no immediate signs i.e. any weight gain, any missed cycle. I was teaching aerobics (high impact stuff) and just went for a check at the clinic… In my mind set I thought that I would never have a child as with all my personal circumstances it just never seemed the thing to do, and not having any relishing memories of my childhood, why would I want to bring a child in to the world?... Chris had two grown up children so nothing was further from his mind either. Yet when I found out, I was a tiny bit excited that God had sent me a gift of a child - the universe stepping in again. I was 11 weeks into the pregnancy and thought Wow, is this really happening at the age of 32?

I was lunching out with a girlfriend (Merlin) when it was confirmed by the clinic and it was hard to take it in at first. How *do* you tell your partner who was 18 years my senior that he's going to be a Dad again...?

So I cooked a romantic meal, which wasn't unusual and told him the news… Shock or what, he didn't speak to me for a month, couldn't communicate at all and when the Mr Nice Guy who I had been with for around 4 years asked me one evening, was there anything I could do about it, I think a part of me stopped loving him there and then.. .

I told him I was keeping the baby and that it wouldn't interfere with his business life and we would get a nanny and build a nanny flat, which is what we did. We did get married soon after with a beautiful wedding and a few months later came our gorgeous daughter who we named Celine Victoria, a French name, as she was (I worked out) conceived in France on a wonderful holiday….. Also I was taking French lessons and the teacher helped me choose her name.

After having borne a child I really did feel complete as a woman and had not envisaged how complete it made me feel. I loved her so much and so did her Dad, Chris. He adored her. I'd never known him come home so often and so early from the business…

This lasted for a couple of years when things started to change. ………….

14. Glamour & Glitz

I received the phone call from Jose whom I had met only fleetingly at my very dear friend Jeans' hotel over dinner. Jose was a PA to two gentlemen whom I had also met through my friend Jean who had known them for a number of years. The boys were successful property developers who every year used to rent a luxurious villa on the West Coast of Barbados right in the heart of Millionaires Row close to Sandy Lane and other prestigious hotels.

The phone call was asking me whether I was interested in sharing a room for two weeks, all expenses paid. (IS the Sky Blue?) One slight problem - I had my husband and a young daughter to consider. But then these invitations don't come along every day.

That night I prepared Chris another romantic meal and approached the subject of the invitation. To my complete surprise he said, "Well you can't miss an opportunity like that. Of course you must go".

Deep down I know he didn't want me to go but how many invitations do you get like that in your life? So there I was on a cold January evening looking forward to spending two very warm weeks in February in sunny, hot Barbados. Was I excited!!!

Jean & Sheila were also going which made me feel that I'd be in great company. They are a laugh a minute with many years experience of how to enjoy themselves and they had known The Boys as we called them for many years.

The chauffeur picked us up very early from the Hotel in the dark and the three of us were taken down to Heathrow. Bacon and egg sandwiches were consumed on the way down followed by Jean's never ending supply of Gin and tonics from her cool bag. She never went on any trip without, the afore mentioned Jean & Tonic, even on a local trip…

When we arrived at the airport we bumped into a couple of other ladies who were also invited and regulars to the holiday, unusual characters to say the least… I didn't reserve my judgement in those days and my facial expressions say a lot! Ros was her name and common was her nature, she was with her friend Jill. Jill was a very bonny bubbly lass who was manageress of a top hotel in London and looked after all the bookings for the chaps. And Ros, I was about to learn...was a hooker.

The plane was over subscribed so we were asked if we would redirect and go to Barbados via New York and guess who I got to travel with... yes the hooker!! in her cheap fur coat and probably no knickers!

Anyway we got on the plane and within minutes she started chatting up some foreign chap. I tried to sleep... No chance…… When we landed in the Big Apple it was freezing. Ros must have had a premonition or something. I mean, why take your fur coat to Barbados?…. Anyway I've never been so cold in my life. I wished I had had a fur coat…

She had a sort of drone that if you've seen the film Airplane (the part that made one of the passengers want to hang up a noose and end it all.) You'll know what it was like. I tried to look at the bigger picture….

Well the holiday was amazing. I saw how the other half really live and wanted more... The West Coast of Barbados

was the place to be. We stayed in a private house called Sara Moon right next to The Royal Pavilion Hotel.
It was the most glamorous two weeks of parties, great company, water skiing, wining and dining, sipping Laurent Perrier champagne from mid morning to midnight in the beautiful Caribbean sun. One day we had not one but two private jets to take us over to Martinique and had a private lunch and fashion show laid on for us. Another day a catamaran with a personal crew took us out cruising in the warm Caribbean Sea... We had cabaret acts from the Sandy Lane hotel come to the house and entertain us one night. I was asked to take part in as a show girl. Guests and celebs came and went all day long... Each morning the water ski guys would pull up at the bottom of the garden right on the beach and ask if they were required? We had a themed red and white Valentines night and danced under the stars... Every day was a party...

It was very hard to settle down to normality in the depths of the grey skies of England. I probably wasn't the easiest person to live with, as all I could think about was being back there...

15. Poison Ivy

Well I settled down again after a while and life became reasonably normal again. We decided to redecorate the bedroom and have it totally refurbished and add on a shower room. After seeing Chris off to work one morning my telephone rang and the voice said quite raucously "Your husband is with your Mother."

Now when you've had a turbulent relationship with your Mother since the day you were born, these are not words you want to hear... I immediately telephoned Chris at work, he wasn't there. My heart sank. I then drove around to my mother's house but remembered somehow that she had recently moved. Little did I know that it was some location that Chris was helping some business colleague out with. I found out some time later when going through a painful divorce that he owned the house and she was renting it from him. Unbelievable... Anyway mobile telephones weren't fashionable then and when I questioned where he had been, I received some cock and bull story. Not only had my mother ruined my childhood she seriously wanted to ruin my marriage. She had made a play for my previous husband and never forgave me for marrying him as she fancied him herself, big time... I could write a book solely on my relationship with my mother. I maybe need to do some more releasing but I have forgiven her in my heart as hanging on to stuff really stops you from going forward.

I've found out many things since but have let it go now and realise people have to live with the way they are. We all have to live with our decisions and thank God that they have to live with theirs. Since then she has tried to poison my daughter but what she doesn't realise is that the only person she has poisoned is herself...! Very sad really. But I once heard a cliché - when you point the finger you point two back at yourself.

So what lesson have you learned from decisions you have made?

16. Millionaires Row

<u>Be careful what you ask for again.. You just might get it or Very Nearly!</u>

Well his name was Gary... let's leave it at that, an American in London not Paris!!!

He was a friend of my third husband (Yes, I squeezed in another marriage. (My best friend Simon and maybe we should have stayed friends...) I think Gary thought he could buy me but as Paul McCartney knows, money can't buy you love … as he himself has proven and I certainly wasn't being bought.

What is it with men and Money! Or women for that matter!!

It can buy you many services and young girls on your arm. You can enjoy the attention and become really deeply fond of them and love what they do but I don't really feel that young women fall in love with those sort of men. You can genuinely love what they do, but I have my own reservations...

Albeit this short duration was brought about when we were invited to dinner at a very sought after London Address and, as Gary was just recovering from a shoulder operation, I thought I would take down some of my magical Japanese magnetic products.

Well we had dinner and Gary was impressed by the products and wanted to know more... At the same time the company had brought out some new pi mag water which helped to strengthen and balance the body.

As Gary had a sister in the states who managed the Calgon Water industry and he also had HUGE connections with all the water companies i.e. Danone Perrier etc in Paris, he requested a meeting with the bosses at headquarters in Milton Keynes together with myself and said this could be the initiation of me becoming a millionairess.

Well we did have the meeting but, and there was a BIG But (I could have kicked somebody's butt!). This was a networking marketing company and it couldn't be sold as a commercial product. Were they having a laugh because I was nearly crying. We were offering to get their product into International companies and they were turning it down! This was my BIG Chance, an opportunity of a lifetime. We did ask if they would ask the big wigs in Japan to get involved.

The next surprise was a letter from Gary propositioning that if the business deal were to come off, then he would expect that we would be more than just business partners and that I would have the lifestyle I was looking for…

In the midst of all this Simon and I had separated for all sorts of reasons... I was hoping it was going to last forever. I suppose now I could have tried harder but felt it was an uphill struggle and I wanted to look up to him and marry him, not carry him... I don't mean that unkindly but I felt all the weight was on me… to support us.

I went to meet Gary in London... for a chat and discussions. On the train down I felt very uncomfortable and kept thinking, what on earth am I doing? Anyway Gary was there to meet me at London, St Pancras train station and we went back to have a chat at his apartment. He duly opened a bottle of Champagne, no doubt to let me unwind. It didn't work. Still I had the theatre to look forward to and we went to see Anything Goes. Maybe the message was in the title.

Afterwards he took me to a newly opened restaurant in Piccadilly where I saw Bill Nighy sitting at the next table (just when Love Actually had been released) and when Gary had gone to the gentlemen's excuse me room, Bill stood up and gave me a gentle bow. Maybe he thought I was someone else. I never found out because Gary came back... As I looked around I saw other young couples obviously in love. Again I thought what am I doing here? Two straws that broke the camels back was one, he asked me for some cash as he hadn't enough to pay the bill which meant then we had a long walk back to the car, then two, when we eventually got to the car it had been clamped. We did get home eventually and I was not amused.

Luckily I feigned being very tired and went to bed - alone! Sensing my discomfort the next morning he asked me if I would like him to get the train timetable home. I was so relieved and cried all the way home.

A few days later I received a romantic home made music CD and a letter of proposal asking me to change my mind and said he would cut me in on a billionaire deal he was working on. He was also having a yacht built which was to be moored at Puerto Fino in Italy and also owned half a castle in Cornwall which I would have rights to. Photographs were enclosed... I said no in a polite letter quoting we could only do business... Was I crazy?
I'll never know!

17. Relatively speaking

When we get an ailment or something breaks down within the body, it's all relative... It is my belief that when something goes wrong within the body it is comparative to what's going on in your life.

i.e. I've a headache... You hear people say: she, he or it is doing my head in …..
I've neck ache – someone is being a pain in the neck
Or if the pain is in the throat area - they need to speak out!!!
Pain in the shoulder: Shouldering responsibility!
Arthritis: Restrictive
Digestive problems: inwardly digesting ….
Eye problems: not willing to see or a situation
Face problems, neuralgia: not facing up to a situation...
Ear ache: not willing to listen … or wanting to hear …..
Water work problems: being pissed off with life or a situation
Bowel & intestinal: Life's crap or feeling sh….
Heart problems: to do with love
Circulation, blood: not going with the flow!!!!!!!!!!!
Knee problems: Need to move forward, getting stuck

You hear people say, "and suddenly she or he got this or that." Well it didn't happen suddenly. It's that they weren't aware of it happening. When the person who is ill is diagnosed it's then they become really worried about it... Suddenly everyone sits up and takes notice. Ring any bells?

18. Dancing Queen

My January was running the normal anti climax route………..

I was in the routine of collecting my daughter from her job at the Holiday Inn... On the way there I decided to listen to the local radio on this particular evening which, I have to say, is unusual for me. It was about a very worried student who had become pregnant (why she got herself pregnant escapes me but there we go again, the old cliché).

The question she was putting out (a desperate plea I would say) was should she keep it or should she have an abortion. Of course from our own life's experiences we will all answer differently... whether through personal experience, peers influence, religion or whatever. It is not a wise decision to put it out to a radio audience!!

For whatever reason I was meant to listen and I mentioned it to my daughter when she got in the car. Her response was interesting as she asked me how I would react in the same situation... My reply was that how can we make that decision for someone else as we don't know the personal circumstances.

Some of the responses of the listeners were as follows:
Get rid of it because your life will be ruined...
Other people are desperate to adopt, so have the baby and put it up for adoption....
One response was murderer. !!
Keep the baby and work around the situation...
It was the local debate of the evening; I generally don't listen to these programmes as they wind people up - including me...

How can anybody know how any one woman is feeling when they find out they are pregnant especially if it's not planned.

I was about to find out!

I picked Celine up a few evenings later and I remember it was a Monday evening. The reason I remember it so vividly was that the previous day I had been at a local health club raising money for a trip planned to Peru for Action Medical Research, believe it or not for a premature babies' appeal campaign.

The same afternoon I also had a telephone call from a dance friend who had asked me if I would consider stepping in at the very last minute to perform an Abba performance at the Blackpool dance championships as one of the group had fallen pregnant (aged 40) and did not want to take the risk of being thrown and twirled around and putting herself at risk from all the rehearsals.

It was an eventful 24 hours… to say the least...
I went dancing on a Monday evening after teaching Aerobics and collected Celine on the way round. I always poured a glass of wine as a wind down when I got home... Celine came into the lounge sat down and blurted out **"Mum"** …. Pause "You know that programme you were listening to the other night when you collected me"…, pause "Well, I'm pregnant". The shock nearly gave me a nervous breakdown on the spot. My head was reeling and the sheer shock of emotion made me react very, very emotionally... It felt too much to bear after the life I had aimed to give her... All the privileges, private schooling, hobbies, quality of life and most of all love. I practically screamed… "Noooooooooooo."

I didn't get it at all and I was distraught... All she could say was "You're not handling this very well, Mum". I could have hit her... But I didn't of course.

On reflection and knowing what I know now I was thinking about myself more than her and was reacting to her situation, I kicked in to the Script Of Life ...

The following evening I turned up at the dance rehearsal my mind was still reeling (my day job did not receive my full attention that day as you can appreciate.)

I was thinking and watching everyone that had been rehearsing since October. What had I let myself in for. They were all so good. In for a penny I thought and, in retrospect, it was a saving grace. I had something to throw myself into for the next four weeks. Amongst everything else I did, it consumed my entire spare thinking time. Everything happens for a reason," - my cliché line.

Well I have to say the team were very supportive. What I haven't mentioned is my ex boyfriend was in the dance team with, his then, new girlfriend showing off .... Luckily I rose above it; he's not with her either now and he's had one or two since then... He's a great dancer though!!! Anyway I threw myself into the rehearsals and was really enjoying it...

In the meantime Celine brought her boyfriend round and they decided to have the baby terminated. That hurt equally as much as finding out about the pregnancy. A secret part of me was relieved or pleased and then I wasn't proud of myself for feeling that way as I feel or know that your spirit or soul lives on... I was selfishly thinking a) for myself and b) for thinking she could get on with her life again... In my solar plexus or gut I felt guilty about being pleased with her decision...

That night I looked in to her room as I always did and saw her sleeping clutching the pink teddy bear she had been sleeping with since birth and I walked out of that room and wept... She was still a child herself in a grown up body... thinking she was an adult..!!!

Well the dance championships were upon us...

We arrived at the Blackpool Winter gardens and throughout the day there were freestyle sessions where you can ask or anyone can ask you to dance...These are good for practice and for forgetting about your nerves. As my ex was there canoodling and showing off, I asked the first man that was passing to have a dance.

Well we chatted, we danced, we flirted... only a little... and later he came and asked me for another dance... His name was John... He was from Edinburgh and the Scottish team were entering the group championships. I let him know the Nottingham team were entering too... Well it came to our slot. Was I nervous or what... blank springs to mind, dry throat and rigid. But hey, nobody knew it was me as I was dressed as an Abba girl in a blond wig. So I went for it...

We came close second and guess who came first - Yes the Scottish team and guess who came over to gloat... But we won the case of champagne and not the money so which team was going to get very tipsy and celebrate their runner up position? You guessed it.

Well the team decided to go back to our very typically Blackpool B&B with a dance floor to celebrate our success... And left!

On arriving back at the hotel, about five minutes walk away, I slipped up to my room and realised I didn't have the gorgeous bracelet I had been wearing so I said to the gang that I would go back to the venue and see if anyone had handed it in. Geoff, my dance partner offered to walk me back but I said no need, I would be back soon and not to worry.

I made my way back up to the venue and went up on stage and asked the DJ if he would make an announcement asking if anyone had seen or found the bracelet... Immediately someone came rushing up with it in their hand. Was I pleased or what... Thanking them I walked off the stage only to bump back into the Scottish dancer (John) who said before you leave you can pop that in my pocket because you are not leaving until you have a last dance with me... I felt like Cinderella without the slipper... After the dance he said that he saw me leave and he didn't have the courage to come and speak to ask me for my telephone number. He than saw me come back and thought this is meant to be and the rest is history. We did keep in touch and had a year long relationship. To this day I still value our time together. Thanks John, xx

Well Celine did have a termination and life moved on. I went to Peru feeling a slight hypocrite all the way though I was hurting, for all of us: Celine, her boyfriend, the baby and me and all of humanity.

And then I was fifty. Bloody hell!

So my message to you is don't wait until you're fifty do it now or if you're over fifty do it now anyway…

Put on your dancing shoes or whatever hat you want to wear. Life's too short to wait.

19. My Wondrous Story

When the phone call came and Richard was asking me to come on The Broadband Consciousness / Super Heroes Course, I thought "Why me?". Then I thought "Why not me?" At the time of asking a shiver went down through my whole body which signifies that it was a sign from the universe to accept... Richard is a fantastic inspirational speaker who delivers seminars all over Europe and this was just 5 people on a 5 day course who were invited to attend. The message to him was build it and they will come, as in the Kevin Costner movie Fields of Dreams. We didn't make a movie. Well, not yet. We just aimed to change a lot of people's lives to help them really believe in themselves. I was about to find out one of the attendees had a burning ambition to be a film maker so watch this space! Since then he is now producing a film with John Hannah and Joanna Lumley. How cool is that!

So what makes a Super Hero? Apparently it needs a lot of research...
If you break it down research is just re - searching and re - searching over and over again.....

I had researched being an unloved child since birth with some physical and mental abuse. A home maker at 13 looking after a dad and a brother after my mother left....
I had researched always feeling I wasn't good enough or clever enough or feeling that I didn't somehow deserve success although I yearned for it...
Of always feeling that everyone was more clever and intelligent than I was...
I have researched 3 marriages and not stayed in any of them.
I've researched being a lover a few times.

I have researched being a mother, an unloved daughter, sister, friend.
I have researched being an employee.
I have researched being spiritual and religious, fitness instructor... complimentary therapist, to name but a few... And now my latest research is accepting my daughter is expecting a child of her own and only nineteen.... huge research that one, I may need help with it although by the time you read this the research will have been done .....

On the first day of the Super hero course we were asked to tell our story, (Beyond Words) and asked to give a summary of our lives. (From the Heart.)! Wow

MY Story... As briefly touched on before:

Born from the outcome of a shotgun marriage, life must certainly have been challenging for my parents... facing the music, parental disapproval etc..
Well growing was not easy for me.
I never experienced being loved or cuddled that I can remember and always felt very sad and lonely, felt that I never fitted in and wondered why I'd ever shown up in the first place and questioned even at a very young age that there must be more to life than this.. I watched other children and envied the love of their mother. I listened to my parents falling out and violence crept in at times...
I grew up in a Coronation style Street where everyone knew everyone with a corner shop and people never locked their doors...
I went to school and just seemed to exist. Apart from the first day I don't ever remember my parents coming to school. In those days all the kids walked to school together. As I got older I always walked by myself.

In my spare time I used to take myself off for walks and dream of how I wanted my life to be and also I used to read a lot so I wouldn't have to speak to anyone..
One of the biggest devastations in my life was not passing my eleven plus. I was a bright child and couldn't understand this. Looking back, I lacked confidence and remember being terrified of the exam. I really feel you should be assessed on your overall performance and abilities. So for the next four years I went to a really rough school and felt like I was in prison... The only subjects I enjoyed were English, sport and cookery.
Girls would rather beat you up as look at you just if you looked at them the wrong way. And they did. Again I thought I'd been put in the wrong place... When it was time to leave I didn't follow everyone into a factory, I told the careers advisor I wanted to work in an office and so I did.. and went off to work at Mcvities and managed to come runner up in the Miss United biscuits competition at 17.
Crumbs, I was not an ugly duckling after all!

20. Taking Off the Mask

People have said to me so many times that I look so together and seem to have my life in order... Looks can be deceiving. Every time I think I'm almost together and reaching an equilibrium...Wham, Bang - the next lesson comes in …….. I don't know if I've ever been together really.

When people ask us how we are we say "Fine" and we know full well that we're not…. You know that feeling when you're falling apart inside…? My new philosophy is to say that I'm amazing but my day is crap. Like people say "What an awful day" when it's raining or bad weather. I say I'm fine but the weather is awful, otherwise you're prophesizing a bad day …. We can choose the way we feel about things in an instant.

When I decided to take off my mask and be the Real Me, life became very different…

I now speak mostly from the heart and not from the head.

I think – no, I feel - that in the past my heart has been pierced a few times and I closed the world out. It's great that I can be the real me and actually like - no **love** - the feeling it brings...

It's made me feel softer and more pliable and it's bringing in a different energy into my life... It's as though I now have WELCOME on my shirt, instead of, "Hey look but don't come too close"...

The only time I would have done that before is if I've had a few glasses of wine and then I would let my guard down… Too far sometimes.

So the philosophy of this is **Its OK to be you**. You don't need fixing. Get yourself round the right people and eliminate all the rubbish in your life…

All my life I'd be looking out there for the answers …
Everyone else seemed to have their life sorted but me… I felt so unhappy and so unfulfilled. I seemed to hang on to criticisms and not compliments and never felt good enough.
Not educated, although I sort of knew I was fairly intelligent.
Not loved-by the people who I wanted to love me.
Wasn't in the right relationship.
Didn't belong or so I thought.
Didn't have the job I wanted.
Didn't have enough money.
Didn't have the right friends.
Always looking for more…

So what's behind your mask…or is your life a masquerade?

21. If only I had Time

Time is the most precious commodity we have but how often do we hear when asking someone to do something - **"I don't have the time".**

What they mean is: I don't want to give the time or I can't be bothered. After all, we all have the same amount of time, it's what we do with it that counts.

All you need to do is take the "t" off the word: can't or don't or won't and what have you got - all positives!

How many times have you heard "there are not enough hours in the day"? What a ridiculous statement.
We should all choose more carefully how we are going to use the hours we have and, guess what - we all have the same. No more, no less and yet many of us think more successful people have more time. Its just that they use time more wisely.

What about time flies? That's our interpretation... I've never seen time flying…….

Madonna's song is Time goes by so slowly, slowly. It appears to when we are unhappy and appears to fly when we are in a happy state because we want to hang on to it and get rid of it when we're not. An example of this is when we're working and we are waiting for 5 o'clock, or the weekend. And then on Monday morning thinking the weekend went so fast…. It's just our interpretation.

What about 'When time stood still'!
A recent experience of this is when my daughter gave birth to her gorgeous baby boy and he was born with the cord wrapped twice around his neck and arrived into the world

blue and not breathing.. Time seemed to stand still for those precious moments until the experienced nurses revived him.

We talk about spending time with someone... How valuable is that? Be careful who you spend your time with because you can never get that time back. It's likened to spending money!! Once it's gone it's gone. I would imagine that more people give their energy to thinking about money than time and yet if you asked someone on their death bed for a revelation. I would pretty much surmise that they would have spent much of their time differently AND money wouldn't come into it..!

There is a song 'If I only had time'... listen to it some time! People have been asked literally on their last days, if they would do things differently. Most say they would which reminds me of the poem by Nadine Stair

If I Had My Life to Live Over (I would pick more daisies) by Nadine Stair

I'd dare to make more mistakes next time.
I'd relax, I would limber up.
I would be sillier than I have been this trip
I would take fewer things seriously
I would take more chances
I would climb more mountains and swim more rivers
I would eat more ice cream and less beans
I would perhaps have more actual troubles, but I'd have few imaginary ones

You see, I'm one of those people who live sensibly and sanely hour after hour, day after day.
Oh, I've had my moments and if I had it to do over again, I'd have more of them. In fact, I'd try to have nothing else

Just moments, one after another,
instead of living so many years ahead of each day.
I've been one of those persons who never
goes anywhere without a thermometer,
a hot water bottle, a raincoat and a parachute.
If I had to do it again,
I would travel lighter than I have.
If I had my life to live over,
I would start barefoot earlier in the spring
and stay that way later in the fall
I would go to more dances,
I would ride more merry-go-rounds.
I would pick more daisies.

Interestingly if you told someone you had just won the jackpot on the lottery and you wanted to give them a share of it, I could guarantee that most people would find the time to come and see you. On the other hand if no one can be bothered to come and see me, or pick up the phone please do not find the time to come to my funeral. I do not want you there, and I mean it!!!

22. Proud mum of a proud mum

Being at the birth of your daughter's baby is an Amazing Experience.

For me is was a de ja vu (Already been) and it could have been me although I was glad it wasn't... Be there if you are invited because it's quite different from the alternative table.

New life, new beginnings, intense joy, raw emotion and a wonderful protection kicks in for your own child giving birth and the new born.

It never ceases to amaze me how a baby knows when to arrive in the world and how the higher intelligence puts everything together. I was at a meeting last night where we discussed life's overall philosophies and experiences and one of the girls said "If I was responsible for putting my daughter together, all the bits would have ended up in the wrong place." So, how does it all network together in a woman's womb?

A few days before the birth, a friend of mine came around to see me and I was still coming to terms with Celine, my daughter, even having a baby, she asked if I had read the chapter in The Prophet (Kahil Gibraan) on Children. Ironically or not because there is no such thing as a coincidence, I said I had a copy in my bedroom having been given it by another friend ....

The chapter quotes "**that our children come through us not from us. They are the sons and daughters of Life's longing for itself**". I recommend you to treat yourself to this small powerful book of liberating thought.

And, what is it about a new born baby that makes us feel compassionate? Is it because it's the closet thing to source, the innocence, and a miracle that we feel empowered, in awe?

Celine and her son, Hayden
Courtesy of Profiles Photography, Nottingham

Is that why we call it Mother Nature because of our protectiveness? Why are our breasts so close to our heart, we feed them from the nearest placing closest to our heart… LOVE - the greatest gift of all …

As a mother we'd rather die ourselves than let anything happen to our children, so why do we send them to war? If they were killed, they're protecting others. We're the ones left with the unspeakable pain!! So why can't we send them to educate and show love to humankind, not into war zones killing, maiming, raping, robbing and pillaging. War does very strange things to minds and it never finishes. It must stay with you for the rest of your life... And our babies are always our babies.

Lambs frolicking in the spring give a lift to the spirits, a crocus or snowdrop pops up, spring is on its way I hear you say. But the reality is that life is changing at an increasing change of knots... Where did that wrinkle come from? It wasn't there yesterday, or those grey hairs. Everything's going south. The extra roll around the middle. You're still doing the same thing and then it appears, a present from God for reaching another birthday.....

23. Dream on

What are your dreams and aspirations? Do you dare to dream, day dream or night dream? Do you go to sleep to escape hoping that life will be different when you wake up? Are you hiding from all the realties? Do you dream of meeting your angels? I ask that my angels take me to a brighter place. Do you go to sleep worrying about your future or celebrating it? I always feel exhausted when I wake up, so I think I have some pretty busy nights, otherwise why don't I wake up refreshed? I always want to stay there for another five minutes and than another five minutes. I feel safe there, away from the big bad world that wants to control us and take all our hard earned cash away…. And when the winter comes bringing the cold dark mornings and the nights drawing in. Brrrrrrr...

If you had a dream what would it be? I'm sure it would be different for all of us….

Do we allow ourselves the privilege of dreaming or do we think that little old me doesn't really deserve it. After all what have I done to change the world?

Start with a single thought or dream, write it down and put a date on it…. Share the dream with someone.

My friend does a dream night where she invites everyone around and asks them to write and paste all their dreams (AND WISHES??) down and put a date on it. It's quite liberating. Then she asks people to look again six months later, then a year. The results are quite surprising. Try it. It really does work. Have a dream night. If they come true even better.

What were your dreams when you were young? and why didn't they transpire into reality?

Do you think we just accept the norm sometimes?

Maybe now is the time to make your dreams come true. Make yourself a list of your aspirations...

....
....
....

24. Sink or Swim

Sink or Swim. Swimming against the tide. Swimming upstream. Life feels like that sometimes. Is it that if it feels too easy then it can't be right? Why is it that we try swimming upstream most of the time and wonder why we find it so difficult? A friend of mine gave a talk about letting go of the oars and really to let go of the side and stop trying to hang on to things that really DONT matter. She talks about the perfect baby being born and we say, "What a miracle". Then - WE take over and try to change everything and think we know best! So, from today, let go of your oars and feel more relaxed and in the flow of life. Stop making it difficult for yourself. There are exciting things around the corner, or just over the horizon, and a few challenges. You're not getting away with it that easily... Another friend quotes that if you accept that fifty per cent of your life will be crap in the scheme of things then you won't be disappointed... Everything will pass, pain and pleasure.

Pay particular attention to what gets on your nerves - family, friends, colleagues, strangers, even people on TV. The universe is sending you signals, letting you know what you have to work on.

We cannot see negativity in someone else unless we have it inside. It's like the negativity inside creates a refracting mirror that lets us see it in other people.

Don't psychoanalyse every reaction, just notice it.
When we worry about something, we create more worry. We don't understand that. How many times do we enjoy something before it happens...? But we certainly worry about things before they happen.

Share your worries without being negative. It's true what they say; a problem shared is a problem halved. Let someone else throw another perspective on it.

But why do we stay with people who don't make us feel good and, even more apparent, why do we think we will change them?

So take a close look at who you're mixing with and don't be afraid to sidestep.

"Create the desire and release the Need"

25. Pushing your buttons...

I first met Tony when a friend took me to see a girlfriend (Sharon) of hers for an astrological reading... Sharon's daughter (Kyra) was in the kitchen and my friend said she would chat to Kyra whilst I had my reading...

The reading was OK and I was told pretty soon I would meet my soul mate. (Hoorah, bloody, hoorah). I have waited a long time. The rest of the cards were good and everything seemed pretty positive...

When we came back into her kitchen, there sat a Liverpudlian pony tailed chap who told me he could see directly into my soul. Spooky or what? I sort of asked myself who these people were. Apparently this was Sharon's ex husband.

A week later he appeared at my place of work with a couple of booooks (Liverpudlian pronunciation) he thought I should read about philosophy. I thanked him and did proceed to read them because my personal philosophy is that everything happens for a reason even though sometimes we can't make head or tail of it.

Anyway he set out to convince me of quite a few things which weren't right in my life but I knew that anyway… At first he became an irritation but on reflection he spoke a lot of sense and I now respect his philosophies. The booooooks he brought for me were amazing and I really understood them. Anyway he turned up at my door quite a few times and said I really didn't get It! He tried to teach me about the Mayan calendar and said that the Gregorian calendar was all wrong. Firstly I didn't understand Gregorian and didn't know The Mayans from Adam.

Sometimes he would turn up on a Sunday morning armed with his guitar and tell me he had written a song about me. He would serenade me in the garden. I think the neighbours thought I'd lost the plot. He tried to teach me some yoga moves… I'm an aerobics instructor and I still find yoga too slow for me. Fitness Pilates suits me better.
He also used to write me poems.

Anyway what I'm trying to say is that divine messages come disguised in all shapes and sizes. He used to really get on my nerves and frustrated the hell out of me. The thing was, when I look back, I envied his lack of responsibility. He made it sound so simple... Everyone you meet has a message and it's usually the ones that irritate you are the ones you need to hear the most.

If I'm really honest I quite envied his freedom and simplicity and that he had nothing to prove to anyone and seemed to survive floating around pleasing himself. After all, isn't that what we all want? It's about letting go again and freeing up space to let the other things float in - I'm learning fast!

The more you empty your mind of rubbish, the more you allow more valuable information to come in...

People come into your life for a reason and push our buttons. Sometimes we don't know why... There is a lesson in there somewhere.

26. Your Roadmap or Sat Nav?

So where do we go from here?

Which direction should we take?
Are you at a crossroads.
How many times have you asked yourself that..?
Only you who are reading this would understand!

Make do with your lot, the others would say sitting in their comfortable lifestyle or dead style...
What are we looking for...?
Lifestyle!
Happiness, peace of mind contentment! Perfect oneness.
Someone to share our life with that's on our wavelength!
Someone to understand us!
Someone to give to..!
Someone to share the moments..!
Where do we go when we leave this life?

As the song says: Do you know where you're going to?
One of my close toastmaster's friends wrote a speech on letting go of the oars. She relates to holding on when life is teaching us to go with the flow and talks of how we cling and cling on to things and people who don't serve us. If she gives permission I'll put it on my website ...
(www.heavenread.com)

So let go of things and people that don't deserve you.
The freedom you experience will be amazing...

Conclusion

I do hope this has given you some insight, inspiration and directive...

I am convinced that we make our lives much more complex than we ought. We are so bombarded with the media downloading information overload. I wonder *if* ignorance is bliss.

If we didn't have a TV or radio or internet or mobile phones and there were no newspapers, what would we worry about? Maybe we'd think more about each other and actually take time to listen. I mean really listen. Isn't that why we were given two ears? Most people jump in on your conversation before you've actually finished speaking instead of waiting for you to finish and then deciding what to say. Most people are already thinking of their reply before you've even finished speaking. After all they're more important and of course they are right... IN their head!

My final question is do you really deserve to be living YOUR dream. Take a moment and send a silent email up to the universal website, stay in the silence and see what your reply is....

Go for it. Enjoy the dream, believe it and it will become your reality.

Judy

Notes

Notes

Notes

Notes

Notes